CENTRAL LIBRARY

SACRAMENTO PUBLIC LIBRARY
D1133245
3 3029 00385 4973

THE ANGEL THAT TROUBLED THE WATERS

AND OTHER PLAYS

BY

THORNTON WILDER

AUTHOR OF

"THE BRIDGE OF SAN LUIS REY,"

"THE CABALA,"

ETC.

PUBLISHED IN NEW YORK

BY COWARD-McCANN, INC.

IN THE YEAR MCMXXVIII

Second Printing

TYPOGRAPHY BY S. A. JACOBS
PRINTED AT THE VAN REES PRESS
NEW YORK, N. Y., U. S. A.

ϒ

CONTENTS

FOREWORD

ϒ

FOREWORD

It is a discouraging business to be an author at sixteen years of age. Such an author is all aspiration and no fulfillment. He is drunk on an imaginary kinship with the writers he most admires, and yet his poor overblotted notebooks show nothing to prove to others, or to himself, that the claim is justified. The shortest walk in the country is sufficient to start in his mind the theme, the plan and the title, especially the title, of a long book; and the shortest hour when he has returned to his desk is sufficient to deflate his ambition. Such fragments as he is finally able to commit to paper are a mass of echoes, awkward relative clauses and conflicting styles. In life and in literature mere sincerity is not sufficient, and in both realms the greater the capacity the longer the awkward age. Yet strange lights cross that confusion, authoritative moments that all the practice of later maturity cannot explain and cannot recapture. He is visited by great depressions and wild exhilarations, but whether his depressions proceed from his limitations in the art of living or his limitations in the art of writing he cannot tell. An artist is one who knows how life should be lived at its best and is always aware of how badly he is doing it. An artist is one who knows he is failing in living and feeds his remorse by making something fair, and a layman is one who suspects he is failing in living but is consoled by his successes in golf, or in love, or in business.

Authors of fifteen and sixteen years of age spend their time drawing up title-pages and adjusting the tables of contents of works they have neither the perseverance nor the ability to execute. They compass easily all the parts of a book that are inessential. They compose dignified prefaces, discover happy quotations from the Latin and the French, and turn graceful dedications. This book is what is left of one of these projects.

The title was to have been *Three-Minute Plays for Three Persons.* I have lately found one of my early tables of contents for it, written in the fly-leaves of a First Year Algebra. Quadratics in those days could be supported only with the help of a rich marginal commentary. Usually these aids to education took the shape of a carefully planned repertory for two theaters, a large and a small. Here my longer plays were to alternate with *The Wild Duck* and *Measure for Measure* and were cast with such a roll of great names as neither money nor loyalty could assemble. The chapter on Combinations and Permutations ended short by several inches, and left me sufficient space to draw up a catalogue of all the compositions I had heard of that were the work of Charles Martin Loeffler. This list of *Three-Minute Plays* was drawn up in Berkeley, California, in the spring of 1915. It contains several that have since been rejected, two that are in the present volume, "Brother Fire" and "Proserpina and the Devil", and the names of many that were unwritten then and that still, through the charm of their titles, ask to be written.

Since then I have composed some forty of these plays, for I had discovered a literary form that satisfied my passion for compression. Since the time when I began to read I had become aware of the needless repetition, the complacency in most writing. Who does not know the empty opening paragraphs, the deft but uninstructive transitions, and the closing paragraphs that summarize a work and which are unnecessary to an alert reader? Moreover, their brevity flatters my inability to sustain a long flight, and the inertia that barely permits me to write at all. And finally, when I became a teacher, here was the length that could be compassed after the lights of the House were out and the sheaf of absurd French exercises corrected and indignantly marked with red crayon. In time the three minutes and the three persons became a habit, and no idea was too grandiose—as the reader will see—for me to try and invest it in this strange discipline.

There were other plans for this book. There was to have been a series of Footnotes to Biographies, suggested by Herbert Eulenberg's *Schattenbilder*, represented here by the Mozart, the Ibsen, and the St. Francis plays. There were hopes of a still more difficult series. Dürer's two sets of woodcuts illustrating the Passion were to serve as model for a series of plays that would be meditations on the last days of Our Lord. Two of them are in this book. There was to have been a series illustrating the history of the stage, and again, two of them are in this book. How different the practice of writing would be if one did not permit oneself to be pretentious. Some hands have no choice: they would rather fail with an oratorio than succeed with a ballad.

During the years that these plays were being written I was reading widely, and these pages are full of allusions to it. The art of literature springs from two curiosities, a curiosity about human beings pushed to such an extreme that it resembles love, and a love of a few masterpieces of literature so absorbing that it has all the richest elements of curiosity. I use the word *curiosity* in the French sense of a tireless awareness of things. (It is too late to arrest the deterioration of our greatest English words. We live in an age where *pity* and *charity* have taken on the color of condescensions; where *humility* seems to mean an acknowledgment of failure; where *simplicity* is foolishness and *curiosity* is interference. To-day *hope*, and *faith* itself, imply a deliberate self-deception.) The training for literature must be acquired by the artist alone, through the passionate assimilation of a few masterpieces written from a spirit somewhat like his own, and of a few masterpieces written from a spirit not at all like his own. I read all Newman, and then I read all Swift. The technical processes of literature should be acquired almost unconsciously on the tide of a great enthusiasm, even syntax, even sentence-struction; I should like to hope, even spelling. I am thinking of some words of Renan commenting in the *Souvenirs d' Enfance et de Jeunesse* upon his education: "*Pour moi, (je) crois que la meilleure manière de former des jeunes gens de talent est de ne jamais leur parler de talent ni de style, mais de les instruire et d'exciter fortement leur esprit sur les questions philosophiques, religieuses, politiques, sociales, scientifiques, historiques; en un mot, de procéder par l'enseinement du fond des choses, et non par l'enseignement d'une creuse rhétorique.*"

The last four plays here have been written within a year and a half. Almost all the plays in this book are religious, but religious in that dilute fashion that is a believer's concession to a contemporary standard of good manners. But these four plant their flag as boldly as they may. It is the kind of work that I would most like to do well, in spite of the fact that there has seldom been an age in literature when such a vein was less welcome and less understood. I hope, through many mistakes, to discover the spirit that is not unequal to the elevation of the great religious themes, yet which does not fall into a repellent didacticism. Didacticism is an attempt at the coercion of another's free mind, even though one knows that in these matters beyond logic, beauty is the only persuasion. Here the schoolmaster enters again. He sees all that is fairest in the Christian tradition made repugnant to the new generations by reason of the diction in which it is expressed. The intermittent sincerity of generations of clergymen and teachers have rendered embarrassing and even ridiculous all the terms of the spiritual life. Nothing succeeds in dampening the aspirations of the young to-day—who dares use the word "aspiration" without enclosing it, knowingly, in quotation-marks?—like the names they hear given to them. The revival of religion is almost a matter of rhetoric. The work is difficult, perhaps impossible (perhaps all religions die out with the exhaustion of the language), but it at least reminds us that Our Lord asked us in His work to be not only as gentle as doves, but as wise as serpents.

The Davis House
Lawrenceville, N. J.
June, 1928.

NASCUNTUR POETÆ

ϒ

NASCUNTUR POETAE . . .

We are gazing into some strange incomprehensible painting of Piero di Cosimo; a world of pale blues and greens; of abrupt peaks in agate and of walled cities; of flying red stags with hounds at their throats; and of lions in tears beside their crowns. On the roads are seen traveling companies, in no haste and often lost in contemplation of the sky. A boy sits on a rock in the foreground. He is listening to the words of a woman dressed in a chlamys that takes on the color of the objects about her.

THE WOMAN IN THE CHLAMYS

In a far valley, boy, sit those who in their lifetime have possessed some special gift of eye or ear or finger. There they sit apart, choosing their successors. And when on the winds toward birth the souls of those about to live are borne past them, they choose the brighter spirits that cry along that wind. And you were chosen.

THE BOY

For what gift, lady, did the choice fall? Am I to mould in clay, or paint? Shall I sing or mime, lady? What choice fell on me and from what master?

THE WOMAN IN THE CHLAMYS

It is enough to know that you were chosen.

THE BOY

What further remains to be done? You have poured on my eyes and ears and mouth the divine ointment; you have laid on my tongue the burning ember. Why do we delay?

THE WOMAN IN THE CHLAMYS

Be not so eager for life. Too soon you will be shaken by breath; too soon and too long you will be tossed in the tumult of the senses.

THE BOY

I am not afraid of life. I will astonish it. Why are we delaying?

THE WOMAN IN THE CHLAMYS

My sister is coming now. Listen to her.

[*The woman in the chlamys withdraws and gives place to her sister whose feet stir not the shells upon the path. She wears a robe of deep and noble red and bears in her hands a long golden chain hung about with pendants. Her face is fixed in concentration and compassion, like the face of one taking part in a sacrifice of great moment.*]

THE BOY

All is ready. What do you come to do?

THE WOMAN IN DEEP RED

My sister has given you the gifts of pride and of joy. But those are not all.

THE BOY

What gifts remain? I have been chosen. I am ready.

THE WOMAN IN DEEP RED

Those gifts are vain without these. He who carries much gold stumbles. I bring the dark and necessary gifts. This golden chain. . . .

THE BOY

[*With mounting fear.*]

Your face is shadowed. Draw back, take back all the gifts, if I must accept these also.

THE WOMAN IN DEEP RED

Too late. Too late. You had no choice in this. You must bow your head.

THE BOY

I am trembling. My knees are hot with my tears.

THE WOMAN IN DEEP RED

Since only tears can give sight to the eyes.

[*She drops the chain about his neck.*]

THE BOY

Then am I permitted to know the meaning of these pendants?

THE WOMAN IN DEEP RED

This is a tongue of fire. It feeds upon the brain. It is a madness that in a better country has a better name.

THE BOY

These are mysteries. Give them no names.

THE WOMAN IN DEEP RED

This is a leaf of laurel from a tree not often plucked. You shall know pride and the shining of the eyes—of that I do not speak now.

THE BOY

And this, lady?

THE WOMAN IN DEEP RED

That is a staff and signifies the journey that awaits you your life long; for you are homeless.

THE BOY

And this . . . this is of crystal. . . .

THE WOMAN IN DEEP RED

That is yours alone, and you shall smart for it. It is wonderful and terrible. Others shall know a certain peace and shall live well enough in the limits of the life they know; but you shall be forever hindered. For you there shall be ever beyond the present a lost meaning and a more meaningful love.

THE BOY

Take back the chain. Take back your gifts. Take back life. For at its end what can there be that is worth such pain?

THE WOMAN IN DEEP RED

[*Slowly drawing back into the shadow of the wood.*]
Farewell, child of the muses, playfellow in the bird-haunted groves. The life of man awaits you, the light laughter and the misery in the same day, in the selfsame hour the trivial and the divine. You are to give it a voice. Among the bewildered and the stammering thousands you are to give it a voice and to mark its meaning. Farewell, child of the muses, playfellow in the bird-haunted. . . .

[THE WOMAN IN THE CHLAMYS *returns.*]

THE WOMAN IN THE CHLAMYS

You must go now. Listen to that wind. It is the great fan of time that whirls on the soul for a season.

THE BOY

Stay a moment. I am not yet brave.

[*She leads him into a grotto and the young soul and his chain are lost in the profound shade.*]

PROSERPINA AND THE DEVIL

A PLAY FOR MARIONETTES

ϒ

PROSERPINA AND THE DEVIL

A PLAY FOR MARIONETTES

A puppet-show has been set up in Venice, 1640 A.D. *The characters of this play are its manager and two manipulators; the puppets are* DEMETER, PROSERPINA, HERMES and DÎS.

THE MANAGER

[*Winningly.*]

Citizens and little citizens! We are going to give you a delicious foretaste of our great performance this afternoon, to which the whole world is coming. This is a pantomime about how a beautiful girl named Proserpina was snatched away by the Devil; and how her mother searched for her over all the hills of the world; and how at last she was able to bring her back to the earth for six months out of every year.

THE FIRST MANIPULATOR

[*Behind the scenes.*]

Let go them strings.

THE MANAGER

At our great performance this afternoon this same play will be given *with words;* and besides it the story of the brave Melusina and her wanderings when she was driven out of Parma.

THE SECOND MANIPULATOR

[*His voice rising in anger.*]

You don't have to show me!

THE MANAGER

On with the play!—but don't forget to bring your rich aunts this afternoon.

[*To the Manipulators.*]

Hurry through with it. I'm off for a cup of wine.

[*The curtain rises with indecent haste and shows the underworld. The rivers Styx and Acheron have been replaced by a circular piece of cloth, sulphur-colored, with waves delicately embroidered about the margin. This is the Lake of Wrath and in it are seen floating arms and legs—all that are left, alas, of great puppets,* ABRAHAM, PENELOPE and JEPHTHA'S *daughter,* MIDAS *and* HARLEQUIN. *Beside the lake* PROSERPINA *is straying, robed in bluish black as one anticipating grief.* PLUTO—*now a medieval Satan—is stealthily approaching her. Suddenly* PROSERPINA *throws up her arms, runs to him and buries her face in his scarlet bosom.* NOAH'S ARK—*mutely protesting against the part it must play, with all its Christianized animals within it, of* CHARON'S *barge—is lowered from the proscenium and the curtain falls.*]

THE FIRST MANIPULATOR

[*Sotto voce.*]

Beard of Medusa! You made her run in the wrong

direction: the hussy courted death. Didn't I tell you he was to chase her three times around the lake?

THE SECOND MANIPULATOR

[*Sulkily.*]

I don't care. A person can't tell which is his right hand and which is his left in this place.

THE FIRST MANIPULATOR

Here, you let me take her; you take the Devil.—Got the orange?

[*When the puppets are next seen* PROSERPINA *is exhibiting grief in pantomime. Her lord with affectionate gestures urges her to eat of a yellow pomegranate. Sadly she puts it to her mouth. With an odd recollection of the Garden of Eden, she tempts him into eating the remaining half. They go out cheerlessly.*]

THE FIRST MANIPULATOR

All right for that. Now I'll take the mother and the Devil. You take the other fellow and the daughter.

[DEMETER, *a handsome Italian matron in a wide gown of brocade, enters with her arms outstretched. At her elbow* HERMES, *the Archangel Gabriel, guides her through the Lake of Perdition.* PROSERPINA *and her husband return and throw up their hands in amazement. Again the frantic girl runs in the wrong direction and casts herself into the arms of Satan.* DEMETER *tries to draw her away, but a matter of pins and hooks-and-eyes prevents her rescue.*]

THE FIRST MANIPULATOR

Oh, you Gazoon! You lack-eyed Silenus! Your hands are nothing but feet.

THE SECOND MANIPULATOR

The Devil take your show and you with it.

[*The altercation behind the scenes grows out of bounds and one blow knocks down the stage. The Archangel falls upon the pavement and is cherished by gamins unto the third generation; the Devil rolls into the Lake;* PROSERPINA *is struck by a falling cloud, and lies motionless on her face;* DEMETER *by reason of the stiffness of her brocade stands upright, viewing with staring eyes the ills of her daughter.*]

FANNY OTCOTT

FANNY OTCOTT

That great actress, MRS. OTCOTT, *an actress in the tradition of the Siddons, the Oldfield, Bracegirdle, O'Neill, is spending a quiet month in Wales. We do not see the cottage; we do not even see the mountains, but there is a stretch of lawn on whose gentle slope there stands an ancient round tower overgrown with ivy. In the shadow of this Arthurian monument* MRS. OTCOTT *has placed a table whereon she is sorting old engravings, playbills, letters, contracts, ribbons—in short, her past. She is still the handsome, humorous, Irish soul from whom every item out of the old trunks exacts its exclamation, its gesture, its renewed indignation or pleasure. She is attended by a blackamoor boy in livery, half asleep against a flowerpot.*

MRS. OTCOTT

Sampson! Tay!

SAMPSON

[*Springing up.*]

Yes, mam. Wid or widout a streak o' cream?

MRS. OTCOTT

Widout. And Sampson, tell Pence I am not at home. Not even to the one in the yellow curls, or to the good black beard. And if they seem to know that I am at home, tell them . . . that I have gone up the tower, or that I have the vapors.

SAMPSON

You wants tea widout, and tell Mrs. Pence you don't want to see none of de gentlemen from de Village Inn,—dat you has de vapors.

MRS. OTCOTT

There! Do you see that, Sampson? I wore that the night the King dined with me on the stage.

SAMPSON

[*His eyes as big as soup-plates.*]

King . . . James!

MRS. OTCOTT

[*Shuddering.*]

No, stupid—Charles.—Go away!—This afternoon I shall devote to another woman, to another and a different woman and yet to myself, to myself, to myself.

SAMPSON

I'll tell Mrs. Pence.

[*He goes out.* MRS. OTCOTT *picks up a packet of letters. One look, tosses them away, then rises muttering, goes and stamps on them and laughs. She returns to pick up a playbill and reads the heading with glistening eyes:* "FANNY OTCOTT *as Faizella in the 'Princess of Cathay.' First time." She strides about lost in thought. She almost walks into a gentleman who has entered through the hedge. He is wearing a black hat and cape, and has a serious worn face.*]

ATCHESON

Your servant, Mrs. Otcott.

MRS. OTCOTT

[*Thunderstruck.*]

Why, *no!* Yes! By the garter, it is George Atcheson. Oh! Oh! Oh!

ATCHESON

I do not disturb you, Mrs. Otcott? I . . . I came to discuss a thing that is very serious to me.

MRS. OTCOTT

[*Suddenly very pleased.*]

Everything is—sit down, my friend. You always were very serious. That's why you made such a bad Hamlet. Delay your serious talk, George, and tell me about the women you have loved since you loved me, and confess that I finally made them all unendurable to you.

ATCHESON

You misunderstand me, Mrs. Otcott. . . .

MRS. OTCOTT

[*Loudly.*]

Fanny.

ATCHESON

Ah . . . Fanny?

MRS. OTCOTT

All you need is a little coaxing. Well, George, a woman drove you on to the stage when you were preparing for the Church, and a woman drove you off, and it was my greatest service to the stage. Look, George, you remember me as Faizella in the *Princess of Cathay*. I never did better than that. Great Rufus, you played opposite me in it. Look!

ATCHESON

Perhaps you remember . . . I lost consciousness. . . .

MRS. OTCOTT

Ah yes! The pale divinity student fainted. Oh! George, you were the first of my lovers. No, it wasn't love, perhaps, but it was beautiful. It was like hawthorn-buds and meadow-larks and Mr. Handel's Water-music. And since, I have never ceased searching for love. Perhaps love strikes the first time or never at all. Then I was too much in love with my work. And oh, George, how young we were! But you were very dear to me in the old garret, and I'm sorry to see you're growing stout, for it's one more reminder that I shall probably live and die without having known the lightning of love.

[*She sits down with a great flow of silken draperies and shakes her head at him ruefully.*]

ATCHESON

I have come to discuss our . . . our association. . . .

MRS. OTCOTT

Thunder and Hell! don't you call that an association!

ATCHESON

. . . but my view of it is very different.

[*Her shoe commences to mark time nervously on the turf.*]

After my retirement from the Stage I resumed my theological studies, and I am now Bishop of Westholmstead.

[*The shoe is now motionless.*]

None of my friends know of that . . . that experience in my life, but it has always remained as a bitter . . . as a distressing spot in my conscience.

MRS. OTCOTT

[*After a pause, very rapidly.*]

I see, you want to make a clean breast of the perilous stuff. You want to make a public confession, probably. You are married?

ATCHESON

Yes.

MRS. OTCOTT

You have several sons probably?

ATCHESON

Yes.

MRS. OTCOTT

And you lie awake nights, saying: Hypocrisy, hypocrisy.

[*Pause.*]

Well, make your confession. But why consult me?

ATCHESON

I have followed your course, madam, and seen the growing admiration your art commands in Court,—I might almost say in the Church.

MRS. OTCOTT

You do not suppose that that revelation would cast any deeper shadow on the good name of Fanny Otcott, such as it is. Remember, George, the months you call sinful. It wasn't love, perhaps, but it was grace and poetry. The heavens rained odors on us. It was as childlike and harmless as paintings on fans. I was a girl tragedienne reciting verses endlessly before a mirror and you were a young student who for the first time had seen a young girl braid her hair and sing at her work. Since then you have learned long names from books and heard a great many sneers from women as old as myself. You have borrowed your ideas from those who have never begun to live and who dare not.

ATCHESON

[*His head in his hands and his elbows on his knees.*] I do not know what to think. Your reasoning is full of perils.

MRS. OTCOTT

Go away and tell your congregations what you please. I feel as though you were communicating to my mind some of those pitiable remorses that have weakened you. I have sinned, but I have not that year on my conscience. It is that year and my playing of Faizella that will bring troops of angels to welcome me to Paradise. Go away and tell your congregations what you please.

ATCHESON

You give me no help in the matter, Mrs. Otcott.

MRS. OTCOTT

Go away. In the name of Heaven, go!

[*Crooked with doubt and hesitation, the Bishop of Westholmstead goes out through the hedge. For a few moments* MRS. OTCOTT *sits on the table, swinging one foot and muttering savagely in an imaginary conversation.*]

[*Reënter* SAMPSON *with a tray.*]

SAMPSON

Three gentlemen waited on you from de Village Inn, but Mrs. Pence sent dem away. She said you was up de tower, mam.

MRS. OTCOTT

[*Showily.*]

Go call them back, Sampson. Tell them I have come down from de tower. Bring up the best box of wine, the one with my picture painted on it. I shall be young again.

BROTHER FIRE

BROTHER FIRE

A hut in the mountains of Northern Italy. ANNUNZIATA, *a peasant woman, is preparing the evening meal over the fire. Her daughter,* ISOLA, *about eight years of age, is playing beside her.*

ANNUNZIATA

Now, now! Not so near. One of these days you'll be falling into the fire and there'll be nothing left to tell us about you but your shoes. Put them on and get out the bowls for supper.

ISOLA

I like to play with the fire.

ANNUNZIATA

What a thing to say!

ISOLA

I'd like to let my hair into it, gently, gently, gently, gently.

ANNUNZIATA

Don't you hear me tell you it's a wicked thing?

ISOLA

Brother Francis says it's our brother, and one of the best things in the world.

ANNUNZIATA

Tchk, Tchk! What makes the starling sing in his cage all of a sudden?

ISOLA

It's Brother Francis himself looking at us.

ANNUNZIATA

Tell him to come in and have some supper.

ISOLA

Come in, my mother says, and have some supper.

[FRANCIS *appears at the door. He blesses the house.*]

BROTHER FRANCIS

I can very well go on to my own supper and need not lighten your kettle.

ANNUNZIATA

Come in, Brother Francis. What you take will not even make a new ring around the kettle. Besides, I see you have been up to the top of the mountain again. You are cold and wet. Come and sit by the fire.

BROTHER FRANCIS

Yes, I have been up to the very top since yesterday, among the rocks and the birds in the rocks. Brother Wind was there and Sister Rain was there, but Brother Fire was not.

ANNUNZIATA

Now you sit by him, Isola, while I get some more wood; but don't ask him any questions. Now, Brother, put this fur skin across your knees.

[*She goes out.*]

ISOLA

What did you do, Brother Francis?

BROTHER FRANCIS

I watched and waited to see what they would let me see. For a long while there was nothing; then they nodded to one another, meaning that it was permitted to me. I watched seven stars closely. Suddenly they turned and fled inwards, and I saw the Queen of Heaven leading forth her company before all the shipwrecked seamen of this world.—However, do not tell thy mother, for she believes in no one's miracles but her own.

ISOLA

My mother says the fire is a wicked thing.

BROTHER FRANCIS

[*Turning.*]

What, Sister Annunziata, how can you say that?—Why, what would cook your broth, what would keep you warm? And when you return from the mountain-tops, what else shines out from all the friendly windows of the world? Look at its flames, how they lean towards us!

ISOLA

It says: Give me something to eat. Give me something to eat.

BROTHER FRANCIS

[*Excitedly.*]

Yes, yes. Its warmth is a kind of hunger. I have a love for all things in fur, feathers and scales, but I have not less a love for the fire that warms us.

[*He edges the cloak into the fire.*]

Look how it reaches for it. Wicked? Wicked? Never.

ISOLA

But, Brother Francis, it will . . . it will . . .

[*The flames suddenly seize the cloak.* FRANCIS *rises, wrapped in fire.*]

Brother Francis, you are on fire! Mother, mother!

[*She rushes from the hut and returns with her mother.* ANNUNZIATA *snatches the fur from* BROTHER FRANCIS *and throws it into the hearth.*]

BROTHER FRANCIS

[*Still standing ecstatically with lifted hands.*]

Eat, Brother Fire. I knew you wanted this. I knew that you loved me too.

[*He looks about him; then ruefully to* ANNUNZIATA.]

Sister, you have spoiled his supper.

ANNUNZIATA

[*With somber and averted face.*]

I do not know what you mean. Here is your bowl of broth. Sit down and eat it.

BROTHER FRANCIS

Sister, do not be angry with me.

ANNUNZIATA

[*Breaking out.*]

Come now, should we kill everything, the animals for their furs, yes, and one another, to feed them to the fire? Is it not enough that it takes our good pine tree by our road? There, that is logic, Brother Francis.

BROTHER FRANCIS

Bring me not logic, sister. She is the least of the handmaids of Love. I am often troubled when she speaks.

ANNUNZIATA

Must we give what makes us often warm, for that which makes us warm only for a moment?

BROTHER FRANCIS

[*Waving his wooden spoon about humorously.*]

My mind is strangely light to-night, like the flames that play about the relics of Saint James. I could wander again through the whole night.

ANNUNZIATA

Where is your mother that she should watch over you? Had I not these other duties I should leave everything and watch over you myself.

BROTHER FRANCIS

She is in Paradise with a golden crook, leading the flames that died of hunger in this wicked world. She leads them to pasture on drifts of dried leaves. Look, Isola, I know that there is flame to burn all evil in the Lake of the Damned. I do not speak of that now,—but I know also that fire is at all times useful to the great Blessed. It surrounds them and they dwell in it. And even now . . .

[*And so on.*]

THE PENNY THAT BEAUTY SPENT

THE PENNY THAT BEAUTY SPENT

The little heartbreak takes place in a rococo jeweler's shop in Paris. The shop is elegantly small and elegantly polished. The few jewels and the few pieces of brocade are tossed from surface to surface in a world of glass, from the chandelier to the mirrors and from the mirrors to the cases. It is Royalty's own place of purchase and the great egotistical head is present in bust and in miniature and on the backs of spoons. The old jeweler, enigmatic and smiling, is suddenly called to the door by a great clatter. A girl enters borne on the shoulders of a boy little older than herself. LA GRACILE *is thin and pinch-faced, but long penury has only made her the more elfin. Illness is already writing its progress in the eyes and on the brow of* QUINTE, *her husband. But they are deliciously happy and full of their secrets.* QUINTE *lifts her onto the counter and draws back.*

LA GRACILE

While you are with me I need never touch the ground. You can carry me from cushion to cushion.

QUINTE

And on your gravestone will be inscribed: Here lies an exquisite dancer, she who never touched the ground.

LA GRACILE

And beside mine yours will read: Here lies her husband, the soul of her life, the sole of her shoes.

THE JEWELER

Mademoiselle is in pain? The feet of Mademoiselle are in pain?

LA GRACILE

[*After she has recovered, with* QUINTE, *from the whirlwind of intimate amusement that this preposterous idea has caused them.*]

No. I am the new dancer. I am La Gracile. Except when I dance I wear nothing on my feet but little velvet pockets. So when I am not wearing my practice slippers, my husband carries me about.

THE JEWELER

Oh, you are La Gracile. We have already heard of your great success last night. The King is delighted with you.

LA GRACILE

[*Shrilly, clapping her hands.*]

Yes, yes, yes. I was a great success. Even the King's favorite, Madame d'Hautillon, was jealous. She tried to stand on my foot. They call me the moth of Versailles.

THE JEWELER

And now the King has sent you here to choose a present for yourself.

LA GRACILE

How did you know?

THE JEWELER

The King sends to me for a gift every young lady who pleases him. Madame d'Hautillon was here last.

LA GRACILE

[*Chattering on.*]

I want nothing myself. It is to be for Quinte. A chronometer, please, that strikes every hour with a gavotte and midnight with a sarabande.

QUINTE

Nothing for me, Claire-Louise. When my cough returns it will shake every ornament off me, the buttons from my coat, the rings from my thin fingers. You must have something in pearls.

LA GRACILE

Silly Quinte, I want nothing.

QUINTE

But I suppose . . . You must wear something for the King.

LA GRACILE

[*Suddenly under a passing cloud of melancholy, resting her cheek on his hair, plaintively.*]

I do not want a great showy pin on my breast. I want only a little white daisy from our beloved Brittany, from Grandmother's field that had too many stones.

QUINTE

Tell her what you have, Monsieur Jeweler.

THE JEWELER

Mademoiselle will look at this chain? Its art is secret. It is painted gold, the work of aged nuns in Hamburg.

QUINTE

Oh look, Claire-Louise, this flower for your hair. Many topazes were splintered to powder on the wheel before this perfect one.

THE JEWELER

Etiquette forbids, Mademoiselle, your buying that; it happens to be the very thing that Madame d'Hautillon bought for herself.

LA GRACILE

[*Arousing herself, imperiously.*]

Have you a little fat chronometer with many jewels in it?

THE JEWELER

[*Proffering a tray.*]

The best in Paris.

LA GRACILE

[*Giving one to* QUINTE.]

That is for you, Quinte, from myself and from the dull King. Like my thoughts, it will rest on your heart, but long after it is sold as wire and rust my love will go on in the land where clocks do not mark off one sad moment from another.

QUINTE

[*With tears.*]
Claire-Louise, it can be of no pleasure to me. In a while it will only please me because it is a little cool in my hot hand.

LA GRACILE

[*Softly, in pain.*]
Courage, dearest Quinte, courage.

THE JEWELER

[*Interrupting formally.*]
Remember, Mademoiselle, that etiquette demands that you will choose a present that His Majesty will admire on you.

LA GRACILE

[*Stormily.*]
I shall choose what I please.

THE JEWELER

[*Insinuatingly.*]
Your life is only to please the King. He has chosen you. By sending you here he is telling you that.

LA GRACILE

You are mistaken. . . . But I am only a poor thin dancer that . . . that has worked too hard. Besides, this is my husband.

THE JEWELER

[*Smiling.*]

No, Mademoiselle, he is not your husband.

LA GRACILE

[*Jumps down and walks away, weeping bitterly, her little feet-sacks flopping against the polished floor. She suddenly turns with blazing eyes.*]

I shall run away to Brittany . . . I shall scratch his eyes out.

THE JEWELER

[*Smiles at this foolish notion and leans across the counter, holding towards her a great jewel-encrusted buckle.*]

LA GRACILE

[*Wildly.*]

Even though all Versailles kill me with steel pins, Quinte shall have the watch.

[*But he has fallen among the gilt chairs.*]

THE ANGEL ON THE SHIP

THE ANGEL ON THE SHIP

The fore-deck of the NANCY BRAY *lying disabled in mid-ocean. The figure-head of the ship has been torn from its place and nailed to the forepost, facing the stern,—back to back, as it were, with its former position. It is the half-length of an angel bearing wreaths; she is highly colored and buxom and has flowing yellow hair. On the deck lie three persons in the last stages of rags and exhaustion:* MINNA, *the captain's wife, the remnant of a stout, coarse woman;* VAN, *the under-cook, a little, sharp youth; and a fat, old, sleepy member of the crew,* JAMAICA SAM.

VAN

[*Driving the last nail into the figurehead.*]
There she is. She's the new gawd of the Atlantic. It's only a she-gawd, but that's a good enough gawd for a sailor.

MINNA

[*Seated on the deck.*]
Us'll call her Lily. That's a name like a god's.

SAM

Youm be quick. Youm say your prayers quick.

MINNA

[*Blubbering.*]
Her can't hear us. Her's just the old figgerhead we had thirty years.

VAN

Her's an angel. Her knows everything.

[*He throws himself on his knees and lays his forehead on the boards. In a hoarse whisper.*]

That's the joss way. We all got t'do it.

[*The others do likewise.*]

SAM

Us'll pray in turns. Us must be quick. There ain't no more water to drink, and there ain't no more sails left to carry us on. Us'll have to be quick. Youm begin, Van. Youms a great lad with the words.

VAN

[*With real fanaticism.*]

Great Gawd Lily, on the ship "Nancy Bray," all's lost with us if you don't bring us rain to drink. All the secret water I saved aside is drunk up, and we got to go over the side with the rest, if you don't bring us rain to-day,—or to-morrow. Youm allus been the angel on the front of this yere ship "Nancy Bray" and you ain't goin' to leave us rot now. I finished my prayer, great gawd Lily. Amen.

MINNA

Great God Lily, I'm the captain's wife that's sailed behind you for twenty years. Many's the time, great God Lily, that I shined your face so you'd look spick and span and we sailing into London in the morning, or into heathen lands. You knows everything, and you knows what I did to my husband and that I didn't let him have none of the secret water that me and Van saved up, and that when he died he knew it and cursed me and Van to hell. But youms forgiven everything and send us some rain or bye-and-bye we'll die and there'll be no one here prayin' to you. This is the end of my prayin', great God Lily.

VAN

[*Whispers.*]
Say Amen.

MINNA

Amen, great God Lily.

SAM

I ain't goin' to pray. I'm just a dog that's been on the sea since I was born. I don' know no land eddication.

MINNA

We all got to pray for some rain.

VAN

You got t'say your word, too.

SAM

God forgive me, great God Lily, I'm old Jamaica Sam that don't never go ashore. Amen. I'd be drowned, too, only for Van and the captain's wife who gave me some of the secret water, so that if they died I could roll 'em over the side and not leave 'em on the clean deck. Amen. Youms known my whole life, great God Lily, and how I stole the Portagee's red bag, only it was almost empty, and . . . and that other thing. Send a lot of rain and a ship to save us. Amen.

VAN

[*Crawling up beneath the figure and throwing himself full-length, hysterically.*]

You've gone and forgiven me everything. Sure you have. I didn't kill the captain. The secret water was mine. Save us now, great gawd Lily, and bring me back to my uncle in Amsterdam and make him leave me his three coal barges.

MINNA

[*Rocking herself.*]

We'm lost. She'll save Sam, but I've done what the gods don't like. They'm after me. They've got me now.

[*Suddenly staring off the deck.*]

Van! Van! Them's a ship coming to us. Van, look!

[*She falls back crying.*]

VAN

Them's comin'!

SAM

[*Trying to jump up and down.*]

It's the "Maria Theresa Third," comin' right at us.

VAN

[*His eye falls on the angel.*]
What'll they say to the figgerhead here?

SAM

[*Sententiously.*]
But that's the great God Lily. Her's saved us. You ain't goin' to do anything to her?

VAN

[*Starting to beat the angel forward with his hammer.*]
They'll call us heathen, bowin' down to wood and stone. Get the rope, Sam. We'll put her back.

MINNA

[*Frightened.*]
But I can't never forget her and her great starey eyes. Her I've prayed to.

THE MESSAGE AND JEHANNE

ϒ

THE MESSAGE AND JEHANNE

The interior of a goldsmith's shop in the Paris of the Renaissance. The tops of the windows are just above the level of the street, and through them we see the procession of shoes, any one of them a novel or a play or a poem. In the workshop one finds not only medals and salad forks for prelates, but unexpected things, a viola d'amore and folios ruled for music.

[TULLIO, *the apprentice, enters from the street and confronts his master,* CHARLES OF BENICET. TULLIO *stands with his back to the door and lets his breath out slowly, as one who has just accomplished a great work.*]

CHARLES

[*Rubbing his hands.*]
So you delivered the rings?

TULLIO

Yes, master.

CHARLES

And what did my little brown Jacquenetta say?

TULLIO

She twice read the verse you had written in the ring. Then she looked at me. Then she looked at the ring. "It is too cold," she said.

CHARLES

Too cold?

TULLIO

She said: "But . . . but I suppose it's what must go inside a ring!" Then she kissed the ring and bade me tell you she loved it.

CHARLES

[*Arrested and puzzled.*]

Too cold, the verse!—But I'll make her another. We forget how they love us. And the other ring? Did you deliver the Graf's ring to the Lady Jehanne herself?

TULLIO

Yes, master. Into her very own hand. Her house is very old and in a bad part of the city. As I crossed the court and stood in the hall a great German, with fierce eyebrows, came in from the street with me.

CHARLES

Yes, that's the one she's to marry.

TULLIO

He asked me loudly what I had there. And I said, a box for the Lady Jehanne, and that it was for her hand alone, and I ran to the landing on the stairs. Then she came out herself. He cried out upon her:

What gift was she receiving? And was it from a certain English student at Padua? And she said: "No, Baron, it is the wedding ring you have sent me." And when I gave it to her she went in, very white, and without speaking to him. Then I went to Jacquenetta's with the other ring, and she gave me some supper.

CHARLES

Too cold, the verse! Start putting up the shutters; I must go and see her.

[*It has been growing darker. Suddenly a pair of shoes, a poem these, descends from the crowd, and* TULLIO *opens the door to a knock. A beautiful lady gives Christian greeting, and a seat is made for her among the littered chairs. She sits in silence until* TULLIO *has lighted the candles and retired.*]

JEHANNE

You are Charles of Benicet, master in precious metals?

CHARLES

Carolus Benizentius auro argentoque magister, and composer of music to God and to such men whose ears He chooses to open.

JEHANNE

You are a composer too?

CHARLES

They are callings like two sisters who have ever their arms about the other's neck. When I have made a wedding ring I compose a motet thereto. The boy who calls to see if the candlesticks are done takes back with him a Mass.

JEHANNE

[*Without a breath.*]

Oh!

CHARLES

Can I serve you with music or with metals?

JEHANNE

You have served me to-day. I am the Lady Jehanne.

CHARLES

Ah, yes! The ring was unsatisfactory? I can make another to-night. I shall set about it at once.

JEHANNE

No, master. The ring is very beautiful.

CHARLES

After a pause, pretending to be embarrassed.]

I am overjoyed that it pleases you.

JEHANNE

[*Suddenly.*]

The verses that you put in the rings—where do you find *them?*

CHARLES

Unless there is a special request, my lady, I put in nothing but the traditional legend: *fidelitas carior vita.*

JEHANNE

[*Without reproach.*]
But there are liberties you allow yourself? Master, what meant you when you wrote within my ring?

CHARLES

My lady!

JEHANNE

[*Giving him the ring.*]
Graf Klaus addresses me thus.

CHARLES

[*Reading around the inside of the ring.*]
"As the hermit his twilight, the countryman his holiday, the worshiper his peace, so do I love thee." It was the wrong ring that was delivered to you, my lady.

JEHANNE

It has broken my will. I am in flight for Padua. My family are truly become nothing but sparrows and God will feed them.

CHILDE ROLAND TO THE DARK TOWER CAME

CHILDE ROLAND TO THE DARK TOWER CAME

The sun has set over the great marsh, leaving a yellow-brown Flemish light upon the scene. In the midst of the mire and among the tufts of iron-grass stands an old round-tower. Its lower narrow door is of green bronze, scarred with many assaults. Above the door are two small windows, behind which a gleam seems to come and go.

In the half-light that hangs over the plain a man in armor stumbles through the bog to the single step before the door. He is many times wounded; his blood flows freely to the ground. The knight blows his horn; the landscape collects itself to listen.

CHILDE ROLAND

I die . . . Open the door to me.

[*The landscape laughs, then falls suddenly silent. Presently its subterranean waters are again heard sucking at buried tree-trunks.*]

I have seen your lights here from a long way off . . . You cannot hide from me now.

[*The marsh becomes animated and fully interested in the stranger. One of the windows brightens slightly and a girl looks out. Her voice and manner are strangely detached and impersonal, as though she had been called away from some absorbing interest, and were eager to return to it.*]

Oh, you are here! Quick, descend to me. All my wounds are flowing. I am dying of thirst.

THE GIRL

Who are you to issue commands against this tower? Some emperor, surely.

CHILDE ROLAND

My name is written with many another upon the sword of Charlemagne: that is enough.

THE GIRL

You are some king, perhaps,—driven into the wilderness by your not too loving subjects?

CHILDE ROLAND

No king, but a friend and soldier of kings.

THE GIRL

Oh! This is some wise counselor. If you are so wise we will quickly open the door to you.

CHILDE ROLAND

Not wise, but often listened to in grave matters, having a voice equal with many others.

THE GIRL

[*Utterly untouched, lightly to some one within.*]

I do believe this is some sweet singer. Let us bind

on our slippers right quickly and put red wine to his lips, for poets are ever our delight.

CHILDE ROLAND

I am no singer, but one loving the string and the voice at all times. Open the door! For the wind is cold on the marsh, and the first terrible stars are stepping into their chains. Open the door, for my veins are emptied on your sill.

THE GIRL

[*Leaning far out, while her red hair falls almost to his shoulders.*]

Beat upon the door, Sir Knight. Many things are gained by force.

CHILDE ROLAND

My hands are strengthless . . . I am fallen on my knees. . . . Pity me!

[THE GIRL *laughs pleasantly to her companion within.*]

Reach over the stars to me, Mary, Mother of God. To you I was committed in my first year, and have renewed yearly my promises. Send from thy golden mind and thy noiseless might the issue out of this difficulty.

[*A second girl, dark and thoughtful, appears at the other window.*]

THE FIRST GIRL

[*Intimately.*]

He is praying now.

THE DARK GIRL

He is a little boy. His thoughts this last hour are returning to his earliest year.

THE FIRST GIRL

Is it not beautiful that a Knight should think of a little child?

THE DARK GIRL

What brought you here, Knight-at-arms?

CHILDE ROLAND

The battle passed suddenly into the west. This tower was all I could see. And here I brought my wounds.

THE FIRST GIRL

[*Softly.*]

You see he is still able to reason; he reasons very well.

THE DARK GIRL

What led you to think that we could help you?

CHILDE ROLAND

I know your name! All my life I have heard of this tower. They say that on the outside you are dark and unlovely, but that within every hero stands with his fellows and the great queens step proudly on the stair.

THE DARK GIRL

And do you believe this?

CHILDE ROLAND

[*After a pause.*]

Yes.

[*With sudden fury.*]

Open the door! There is a place for me within. Open the door, Death!

THE FIRST GIRL

[*Drawing up her hair languidly.*]

He is irresistible, this great man.

CHILDE ROLAND

Oliver! Oliver! Charlemagne! I hear your voices. It is I, Roland, without, in the dark marsh. My body I cast away for you. My breath I returned to the sky in your defense. Open the door! . . .

[*The marsh is a little put out by all this strong feeling. It lies quiet. The door slowly opens upon a hall full of drifting violet mists, some of which escape and fade over the marsh. The girl with the red hair is seen walking away in the hall, her mocking face looking back over her shoulder. The dark girl, robed in gray, leans across the threshold extending a chalice to the Knight's lips.*]

THE DARK GIRL

Take courage, high heart. How slow you have been to believe well of us. You gave us such little thought while living that we have made this little delay at your death.

CENTAURS

CENTAURS

The usual chattering audience of our theaters is waiting for the curtains to part on a performance of Ibsen's THE MASTER BUILDER. *Presently the lights are lowered to a colored darkness, and the warm glow of the footlights begins again the ancient magic. The orchestra draws its bows soothingly to a gradual close and files out gropingly into the rabbit-hutch prepared for it, leaving perhaps a sentimental viola-player staring upward into the darkness. Suddenly the curtains are parted by an earnest young man, who stares into the shadowy audience and starts, with some difficulty, to address it.*

SHELLEY

My name is Shelley. I . . . I am told that some of you may have heard of me, may even know my poems,—or some of my poems. I cannot imagine what they may seem like to you who live in this world that . . . that is, I have just seen your streets for the first time,—your machines, your buildings, and especially the machines with which you talk to one another. My poems must seem very strange in a world of such things.

[*Awkward pause.*]

Well, I wanted to say something about this play,

but I don't know how to put it into words for you. You see, I feel that, in part, I wrote this play.

[*With sudden relief calling back through the curtains.*]

Hilda! Will you help me a moment?

HILDA WANGEL'S VOICE

Yes, I'm coming.

SHELLEY

[*Constrainedly, to the audience.*]

A friend of mine.

HILDA

[*Appears in her mountaineering costume of the First Act, carrying an alpenstock. Vigorously, to the audience.*]

He promised to do this by himself, but he has gotten into difficulties. Have you told them that you wrote it?

SHELLEY

I tried to. It didn't sound reasonable.

HILDA

Well, you were able to explain it to me. Help me to persuade Papa to come out here.

[*She disappears.*]

SHELLEY

Hendrick, for my sake.

HILDA'S VOICE

There, did you hear that? For his sake, he said. Miss Fosli, will you kindly push forward the wicker settee from the last act? Thank you.

[*A wicker settee suddenly appears.*]

Now, Papa.

[*Hilda reappears leading the dramatist. Ibsen is smiling sternly through his spectacles and through his fringe of up-curling white whiskers.*]

Now sit down and Shelley will begin again.

IBSEN

Hurry, young man. My beautiful play is ready to begin. The kingdom is on the table, the nurseries are empty, and this house is full of unconverted people.

HILDA

[*Touching his shoe with the tip of her alpenstock.*]

Hush, Papa. Let him go about it in his own way. Have you told them about the poem you were about to write when you died?

SHELLEY

No.

[*To the audience.*]

Ladies and Gentlemen, on the day I died,—drowned in the Mediterannean,—I was full of a poem to be called THE DEATH OF A CENTAUR, that I did not have time to put on paper.

HILDA

You forgot to say that it was a very good poem.

SHELLEY

I couldn't say that.

HILDA

You said it to me.

[*Turning to the audience.*]

You should know that this young man had come to a time when everything he wrote was valuable. He was as sure to write great poems as a good apple tree it to give good apples.

SHELLEY

Perhaps it would have been one of the better ones. At all events, it was never written. . . .

IBSEN

[*Rising excitedly and stamping his feet as though they had snow on them.*]

And I claim that I wrote it. The poem hung for a while above the Mediterannean, and then drifted up toward the Tyrol and I caught it and wrote it down. And it is THE MASTER BUILDER.

HILDA

Now you must sit down, Papa, and keep calm. We must reason this out calmly. In the first place, both are certainly about centaurs. What do you say, Shelley?

SHELLEY

Well, it is not a strange idea, or a new one, that the stuff of which masterpieces are made drifts about the world waiting to be clothed with words. It is a truth that Plato would have understood that the mere language, the words of a masterpiece are the least of its offerings. Nay, in the world we have come into now, the languages of the planet have no value; but the impulse, the idea of "Comus" is a miracle, even in heaven. Let you remember this when you regret the work that has been lost through this war that has been laid upon your treasurable young men. The work they might have done is still with you, and will yet find its way into your lives and into your children's lives.

IBSEN

Enough, enough! You will be revealing all the mysteries soon. Enough has been said to prove that THE DEATH OF A CENTAUR and THE MASTER BUILDER are the same poem. Get in with you, children. The play is ready to start. Solness sits with his head in his hands and the harps are in the air.

[*He goes behind the curtains. Shelley lingers a moment; a shadow has fallen across his face.*]

HILDA

[*Laying her hand on his arm.*]

What is the matter?

SHELLEY

That reminded me . . . of another poem . . . I did not write down.

LEVIATHAN

LEVIATHAN

MID-MEDITERRANEAN. *Sunrise after a night of storm with the sea swaying prodigiously. A great Venetian argosy has been wrecked overnight; ships and men have disappeared, leaving only the cargo spread out upon the waters. Momently new treasures from the ship's holds float upward and, reaching the surface, are swept hither and thither for miles: Persian rugs, great lengths of brocade, boxes of spice, made from tropical leaves and bound with dried vine; and an apparently interminable swathe of gray silk unwinding from its ivory standard.*

In the foreground a mermaid is feeling her way among the stuffs with considerable distaste. To one used to the shadowed harmonies of deep-sea color these crimsons and oranges have no attraction. BRIGOMEÏDÉ *has the green wiry hair of her kind, entangled with the friendly snail; the iridescent shoulders of all sea-women, and the gray thin mouth.*

Suddenly she comes upon THE PRINCE. *The royal divan has been swept from the decks, and while the huge pillows are gradually soaking up the water and floating away, their Prince lies on them unconscious. For a moment the mermaid watches him open-mouthed. She steals nearer and holding on to the tassels of seed-pearls, leans cautiously over and scans his face long and wonderingly. She sighs faintly, splashes a little in discontent, and then gazes upon him again with a frown of concentration.*

BRIGOMEÏDÉ

It's breathing. He has not lost—what they call—the soul. I wonder where he keeps it. It is the great difference between us; we sea-people have no soul. I wonder where he keeps it! I have heard that it can be seen at times, in the eyes. Perhaps if I borrowed it from him while he slept he would never miss it. No,—I will ask him for it.

[*She claps her hands suddenly to awake him, falling back, at the same time, into the water. The young man does not stir. She grows angry. She strikes the water sharply with the palms of her hands. By quick degrees a circling wind rises; great fantastic waves rear themselves, robed in silk; they break over the divan and the Prince stirs. Immediately* BRIGOMEÏDÉ *strokes the water to a stillness, and fixes her attention on the young man.*]

THE PRINCE

My father, take not your hand away. My brothers, why have you ceased talking? Where am I?—All is lost! *Ave Maris Stella!*

BRIGOMEÏDÉ

[*Watching him intently.*]

How could sleep so—during the storm?

THE PRINCE

You—you are out of a dream. You are out of my fever. Yes, yes—the storm—you—all this is but the painting of my fever. I shall awake in Venice with the lute-player fallen asleep by the window. I will call to him now and he will wake me up: Amedeo!—Lute-player! Shake me out of this dream!

[*The silence that follows is filled with the crackling noise as the pith fillings of the heavier cushions become saturated.*]

BRIGOMEÏDÉ

[*Harshly.*]

Who is it you are calling to? There is no one here, but you and me only.

THE PRINCE

Amedeo!—he does not answer: this is real. But you, you are dream; you are illusion. *Ave Maris Stella!*

BRIGOMEÏDÉ

[*Indignantly.*]

I am not dream. I am not illusion. I am royal among all sea-women—I am of the Third Order; on the three great tide days I am permitted to bind my hair with Thetis-Agrandis and wear in my ears the higher Muria.

THE PRINCE

You are out of an old ballad, taught me as a boy, and you have come back to me in the last hour on the tide of fever. In a moment my dream will have passed on from you.

BRIGOMEÏDÉ

[*Vehemently.*]
You think I am only dream because . . . you have heard it said . . . we sea-folk have no souls.

THE PRINCE

Soul nor body.

BRIGOMEÏDÉ

[*More softly.*]
Tell me where it is you keep your soul. Have you it always with you?

THE PRINCE

[*As a great pillow floats away from under his hand.*]
Flos undarum! Save me! Deliver me! Hear my prayer!

BRIGOMEÏDÉ

Who are you speaking to? Did I not tell you there was no one here but you and me only?

THE PRINCE

You! Tell me we where is shore. You can swim for days. Draw me to some island. I will give you great riches . . . all you desire.

BRIGOMEÏDÉ

Give me your soul. All my days I have longed for two things, black hair and a soul. I have not lacked anything else. I will draw you to your home, if you will give me your soul.

THE PRINCE

[*Violently.*]

It cannot be given away. No one has seen it; it cannot be felt with hands; seen or tasted.

BRIGOMEÏDÉ

And yet they say it is the greatest thing in the world; that without it life is a cold procession of hours; that it gives all sight to the eyes, and all hearing to the ears . . . you are mocking me! I see in your face that you have it now!

THE PRINCE

Yes, and am about to lose it.

BRIGOMEÏDÉ

Give it to me, and I will bring up from the bottom of the sea your father and your brothers. I will return to you all the pearls that have fallen here, and draw you softly into the narrows of Venice.

THE PRINCE

[*As the water closes over him.*]

Amedeo! . . . Lute-player!

[BRIGOMEÏDÉ *turns away contemptuously.*]

BRIGOMEÏDÉ

It is something you cannot touch or see. What could I do with it so?

[THE PRINCE *rises, dead, entangled in scarves.* BRIGOMEIDÉ *stares into his face long and earnestly.*]

It is true! There is something gone . . . that lay

about his eyes, that troubled his mouth. The soul, perhaps.

[*She claps her hands. From a great distance a sea-serpent swims hugely towards her. He is caught in the trailing lengths of gray brocade.*]

BRIGOMEÏDÉ

Gog-etar! There is no longer anything precious in this man. You may divide him among your young.

LEVIATHAN

It is terrible here, lady. These spices have made the streams unendurable. By to-morrow morning the waters will be tainted as far as Africa. Already my young are ill, lady. They lie motionless in the mud, dear lady. It is terrible to see them so. . . .

BRIGOMEÏDÉ

I do not want to hear your troubles. Take this man away.

LEVIATHAN

Thanks, gracious lady. Perhaps these hateful essences will have made him endurable . . .

BRIGOMEÏDÉ

Cease!

[*He drags* THE PRINCE *away. The frustrated* BRIGOMEÏDÉ *starts to comb the shell out of her hair, singing. Suddenly she breaks her song and adds musingly.*]

Perhaps it is better, although your body has passed to Leviathan, still to have another part of you somewhere about the world.

AND THE SEA SHALL GIVE UP ITS DEAD

AND THE SEA SHALL GIVE UP ITS DEAD

The clangor of Judgment Day's last trumpet dies away in the remotest pockets of space, and time comes to an end like a frayed ribbon. In the nave of creation the diaphanous amphitheater is already building for the trial of all flesh. Several miles below the surface of the North Atlantic, the spirits of the drowned rise through the water like bubbles in a neglected wine-glass.

A WOMAN

[*To the gray weeds of whose soul still cling the vestiges of color, some stained purples and some wasted reds.*]

At last I could struggle no longer. My head and lungs were under intense discomfort by reason of the water with which they were filled. I said to myself: "Only think, Gertruda, you have actually arrived at the moment of death!" Even then I was unwilling to believe it, though my lungs were on the point of bursting. One is never really able to believe that one will die. It is especially difficult for sovereigns who seldom, if ever, confront inevitable situations. Perhaps you know that I am Gertruda XXII, Empress of Newfoundland from 2638 to 2698?

A STOUT LITTLE MAN

Your Imperial Highness's experience is much like mine. I lived about five hundred years before Your Imperial Highness. I had always dreaded the moment of extinction, yet mine was less painful than a headache.

THE EMPRESS

We know now that the real pain comes to us in the ages that have passed since then. Have you too been swinging in mid-ocean, tangled in a cocoon of seaweed, slowly liberating your mind from the prides and prejudices and trivialities of a life-time? That is what is painful.

THE LITTLE MAN

I was a Jew and very proud of my race. Living under what I took to be the aspersions of my neighbors I had nourished the arrogant delusion that I was notable. It has taken me five hundred years of painful reflection to disembarrass myself of this notion. I was a theatrical producer and thought myself important to my time, wise, witty, and kindly. Each of these ideas I have shed with a hundred times the pain of losing a limb. Now I am reconciled tc the fact that I am naked, a fool, a child.

THE EMPRESS

In my life I believed fiercely that everything of which I said MY had some peculiar excellence. It was impossible to imagine a citizen proud of any country save Newfoundland, or a woman vain of any hair save the golden. I had a passion for genealogies and antiquities and felt that such things merely looked forward to myself. Now these many years I have been wrapped in barnacles, divorcing my soul from all that it once loved. Even my love for my son and my son's love for me have vanished through sheer inconsequence. All this is the second death, and the one to be dreaded. I was afraid that when I had shed away my royalty and my beauty and my administrative talent and my pure descent and my astonishing memory for names, I was afraid that there would be nothing left. But fortunately, underneath all this litter I have found a tiny morsel of . . . but dare we say the Name?—But what was yours?

THE LITTLE MAN

Horatio Nissem.

THE EMPRESS

Speak to that man who is rising through the water beside you.

HORATIO NISSEM

Who are you, and what particular follies have you laid aside?

A TALL THIN DREAMY MAN

I was a priest of the gospel and a terrible time I have had taking leave of my sins. I tremble to think how but a few moments ago I still retained a longing for

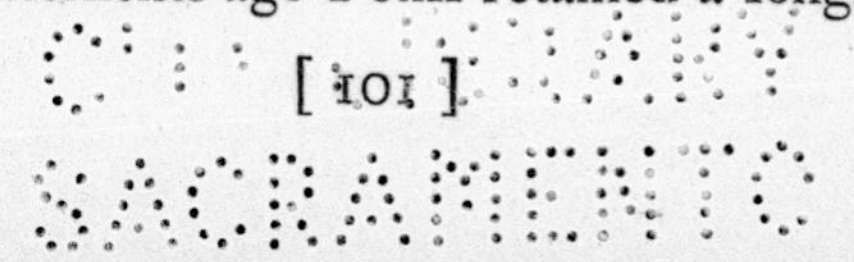

stupidities. Yes, sir, for the planets. I felt sure that they had personalities and I looked forward after my death to hearing their songs. Now I know that sun and moon and stars have fallen like dust into the lap of their maker. I told myself, also, that after death I should sit through eternity overhearing the conversation of Coleridge and Augustine and Our Lord; there I should embrace my loved ones and my enemies; there I should hear vindicated before the devils the great doctrines of Infant Baptism and Sacramental Confession. Only now have I been delivered from these follies. As I swayed in the meteoric slime I begged God to punish me for certain sins of my youth, moments I well remembered of rage and pride and shame. But these seemed of no importance to him: he seemed rather to be erasing from my mind the notion that my sins were of any consequence. I see now that even the idea that I was capable of sinning was a self-flattery and an impertinence. My name was Father Cosroe: now my name is Worm.

THE EMPRESS

We still cling obstinately to our identity, as though there were something valuable in it. This very moment I feel relics of pleasure in the fact that I am myself and no one else. Yet in a moment, if there is a moment, we shall all be reduced to our quintessential matter, and you, Mr. Nissem, will be exactly indistinguishable from me. God Himself will not be able to tell the Empress of Newfoundland from the Reverend Doctor Cosroe.

HORATIO NISSEM

[*In mounting terror.*]
I am afraid. I refuse to give myself up.

THE EMPRESS

Do not cry out, fool. You have awakened all my rebellious nature. O God, do not take away my identity! I do not ask for my title or my features; do not take away my myself!

HORATIO NISSEM

Do you hear? I refuse to give myself up. O God, let me not be mistaken for a Gentile.

FATHER COSROE

Your screaming has aroused my madness. Let me keep my particular mind, O God, my own curious mind with all I have put into it!

[*The three panic-stricken souls reach the surface of the sea. The extensive business of Domesday is over in a twinkling and the souls divested of all identification have tumbled, like falling stars, into the blaze of unicity. Soon nothing exists in space but the great unwinking eye, meditating a new creation.*]

NOW THE SERVANT'S NAME WAS MALCHUS

NOW THE SERVANT'S NAME WAS MALCHUS

In his father's house are many mansions, and it is from the windows of one of them that he stands looking out upon the clockwork of the skies. With the precision that is possible only to things dead in themselves, the stars weave incessantly their interlocking measures. At intervals the blackest pockets of space give birth to a nebula, whirling in new anguish, but for the most part the sky offers only its vast stars, eased in the first gradations of their cooling, and fulfilling happily and with a faint humming sound the long loops of their appointment.

[*To him comes* GABRIEL, *secretary and soldier.*]

GABRIEL

There are some unusually urgent petitions here. . . . There's this Colonel on a raft in the Bengal Sea—Here again is the widow and her two daughters in Moscow. A lady in Rome.

[*He lays some papers on the table.*]

Besides, there is someone outside who wishes to speak to you. He says he knew you on earth. I think he has something to complain of, even here.

OUR LORD

Let him wait a moment.

[*There is loud rapping at the door.*]

GABRIEL

There he is again.

OUR LORD

Then let him in.

[GABRIEL *admits* MALCHUS *and goes out.*]

MALCHUS

Please, sir, excuse me being so hasty, but I had to speak to you about something.

OUR LORD

You are displeased with Heaven?

MALCHUS

Oh no, sir—except for one thing.

OUR LORD

We will talk about it in a minute. Come by the window and look. Can you tell me which of those stars is mine?

MALCHUS

Lord, all are yours, surely.

OUR LORD

No, only one is mine, for only one bears living things upon it. And where there is no life I have no power. All the stars save one are lifeless; not even a blade of grass pushes through their powder or their flame. But one of them is so crowded with event that Heaven itself is scarcely able to attend to its needs. —But you are not interested?

MALCHUS

Oh, sir, it was so long ago that I was there that I cannot be expected to. . . . Even my children's children have long since left it. I cannot be very interested. Since I am so happy here,—except for one thing. But I should like to see it again. Which is it, sir?

OUR LORD

There, see! See where it floats for a moment out of a green mist. If your ears were accustomed to it as mine are, you would hear what I hear: the sigh as it turns. Now what is it you want of me?

MALCHUS

Well, as you know I was the High Priest's servant in the garden when you were taken. Sir, it's hardly worth mentioning.

OUR LORD

No, no. Speak out.

MALCHUS

And one of your fellows took out his sword and cut off my ear.

OUR LORD

Yes.

MALCHUS

It's . . . it's hardly worth mentioning. Most of the time, Lord, we're very happy up here and nothing disturbs us at our games. But whenever someone on earth thinks about us we are aware of it, pleasantly or unpleasantly. A sort of something crosses our mind. And because I'm in your book someone is always reading about me and thinking about me for a moment, and in the middle of my games I feel it. Especially at this season when your death is celebrated, no moment goes by without this happening. And what they think is, that I'm ridiculous.

OUR LORD

I see. And you want your name to be erased from the book?

MALCHUS

[*Eagerly.*]

Yes, sir. I thought you could just make the pages become blank at that place.

OUR LORD

Now that you have come here everything that you wish is granted to you. You know that.

MALCHUS

Yes, sir; thank you, sir.

OUR LORD

But stay a minute. At this season, Malchus, a number of people are thinking of me, too.

MALCHUS

Yes, Lord, but as good, as great . . .

OUR LORD

But, Malchus, I am ridiculous too.

MALCHUS

Oh, no, no!

OUR LORD

Ridiculous because I suffered from the delusion that after my death I could be useful to men.

MALCHUS

They don't say that!

OUR LORD

And that my mind lay under a malady that many a doctor could cure. And that I have deceived and cheated millions and millions of souls who in their extremity called on me for the aid I had promised.

They did not know that I died like any other man and their prayers mounted into vain air, for I no longer exist. My promises were so vast that I am either divine or ridiculous.

[*Pause.*]

Malchus, will you stay and be ridiculous with me?

MALCHUS

Yes, sir, I'll stay. I'm glad to stay. Though in a way I haven't any right to be there. I wasn't even the High Priest's servant; I only held his horse every now and then. And . . . and I used to steal a little, —only you've forgiven me that. Sure, I'm glad to stay.

OUR LORD

Thank you, Malchus.

MALCHUS

[*Smiling.*]

It isn't even true in the book. It was my left ear and not my right.

OUR LORD

Yes, the book isn't always true about me, either.

MALCHUS

Excuse my troubling you, sir. Good day.

OUR LORD

Good day, Malchus.

[MALCHUS *goes out.* GABRIEL *enters discreetly and lays down some more papers.*]

GABRIEL

[*In a low voice.*]
The raft has capsized, sir, on the Bengal Sea, and the Colonel will be here at once. The woman in Moscow. . . .

MOZART AND THE GRAY STEWARD

MOZART AND THE GRAY STEWARD

MOZART *is seated at a table in a mean room in Vienna orchestrating the "Magic Flute." Leaves of ruled paper are strewn about the floor. His wife enters in great excitement.*

CONSTANZE

There's someone come to see you, someone important. Pray God, it's a commission from Court.

MOZART

[*Unmoved.*]

Not while Salieri's alive.

CONSTANZE

Put on your slippers, dear. It's some one dressed all in gray, with a gray mask over his eyes, and he's come in a great coach with its coat of arms all covered up with gray cloth. Pray God, it's a commission from Court for a *Te Deum* or something.

[*She tidies up the room in six gestures.*]

MOZART

Not while Salieri's alive.

CONSTANZE

But, now, do be nice, 'Gangl, please. We must have some money, my treasure. Just listen to him and say "yes" and "thank you" and then you and I'll talk it over after he's gone.

[*She holds his coat.*]

Come, put this on. Step into your slippers.

MOZART

[*Sighing.*]

I'm not well. I'm at home. I'm at work. There's not a single visitor in the whole world that could interest me. Bring him in.

CONSTANZE

[*Adjusting his stock.*]

Now don't be proud. Just accept.

[*She hurries out and presently reënters preceding the visitor. The visitor is dressed from head to foot in gray silk. His bright eyes look out through the holes in a narrow gray silk mask. He holds to his nose a gray perfumed handkerchief. One would say: an elegant undertaker.*]

THE GRAY STEWARD

Kappelmeister Mozart, *servus*. Gracious lady, *servus*.

MOZART

Servus.

THE GRAY STEWARD

Revered and noble master, wherever music reigns, wherever genius is valued, the name of Wolfgang Amadeus Mozart is . . .

MOZART

Sir, I have always been confused by compliments and beg you to spare me that mortification by proceeding at once to the cause of your visit . . . the . . . the honor of your visit.

THE GRAY STEWARD

Revered master, before I lay my business before you, may I receive your promise that—whether you accept my commission or not—you both will . . .

MOZART

I promise you our secrecy, unless our silence would prove dishonorable to me or injurious to some one else. Pray continue.

THE GRAY STEWARD

Know then, gracious and revered genius, that I come from a prince who combines all the qualities of birth, station, generosity and wisdom.

MOZART

Ha! a European secret.

THE GRAY STEWARD

His Excellency moreover has just sustained a bitter misfortune. He has lately lost his wife and consort, a lady who was the admiration of her court and the sole light of her bereaved husband's life. Therefore, his Excellency, my master, commissions you to compose a Requiem Mass in honor of this lady.

He asks you to pour into it the height of your invention and that wealth of melody and harmony that have made you the glory of our era. And for this music he asks leave to pay you the sum of four hundred crowns,—two hundred now, and the second two hundred crowns when you deliver the first four numbers.

MOZART

Well, Constanze, I must not be proud.

THE GRAY STEWARD

There is but one proviso.

MOZART

Yes, I heard it. The work must represent the height of my invention.

THE GRAY STEWARD

That was an easy assumption, master. The proviso is this: You shall let his Excellency have this music as an anonymous work, and you shall never by any sign, by so much as the nod of your head, acknowledge that the work is yours.

MOZART

And his Excellency is not aware that the pages I may compose at the height of my invention may be their own sufficient signature?

THE GRAY STEWARD

That may be. Naturally my master will see to it that no other composer will ever be able to claim the work as his.

MOZART

Quick, give me your paper and I will sign it. Leave your two hundred crowns with my wife at the foot of the stairs. Come back in August and you will have the first four numbers. *Servus. Servus.*

THE GRAY STEWARD

[*Backing out.*]

Servus, master. *Servus*, madame.

[CONSTANZA *returns in a moment and looks anxiously towards her husband.*]

CONSTANZE

A visit from Heaven, 'Gangl. Now you can go into the country. Now you can drink all the Bohemian water in the world.

MOZART

[*Bitterly.*]

Good. And just at a time when I was contemplating a Requiem Mass. But for *myself*. However, I must not be proud.

CONSTANZE

[*Trying to divert him.*]

Who can these people be? Try and think.

MOZART

Oh, there's no mystery about that. It's the Count von Walsegg. He composes himself. But for the most part he buys string quartets from us; he erases the signatures and has them played in his castle. The courtiers flatter him and pretend that they have guessed him to be the composer. He does not deny it. He tries to appear confused. And now he has succeeded in composing a Requiem. But that will reduce my pride.

CONSTANZE

You know he will only be laughed at. The music will speak for itself. Heaven wanted to give us four hundred crowns—

MOZART

And Heaven went about it humorously.

CONSTANZE

What was his wife like?

MOZART

Her impudences smelt to Heaven. She dressed like a page and called herself Cherubin. Her red cheeks and her black teeth and her sixty years are in my mind now.

CONSTANZE

[*After a pause.*]

We'll give back the money. You can write the music, without writing it for them.

MOZART

No, I like this game. I like it for its very falseness. What does it matter who signs such music or to whom it is addressed?

[*He flings himself upon the sofa and turns his face to the wall.*]

For whom do we write music?—for musicians? Salieri!—for patrons? Von Walsegg!—for the public? The Countess von Walsegg! I shall write this Requiem, but it shall be for myself, since I am dying.

CONSTANZE

My beloved, don't talk so! Go to sleep.

[*She spreads a shawl over his body.*]

How can you say such things? Imagine even thinking such a thing! You will live many years and write countless beautiful pages. We will return the money and refuse the commission. Then the matter will be closed. Now go to sleep, my treasure.

[*She goes out, quietly closing the door behind her.* MOZART, *at the mercy of his youth, his illness and his genius, is shaken by a violent fit of weeping. The sobs gradually subside and he falls asleep. In his dream* THE GRAY STEWARD *returns.*]

THE GRAY STEWARD

Mozart! Turn and look at me. You know who I am.

MOZART

[*Not turning.*]

You are the steward of the Count von Walsegg. Go tell him to write his own music. I will not stain my pen to celebrate his lady, so let the foul bury the foul.

THE GRAY STEWARD

Lie then against the wall, and learn that it is Death itself that commissions. . . .

MOZART

Death is not so fastidious. Death carries no perfumed handkerchief.

THE GRAY STEWARD

Lie then against the wall. Know first that all the combinations of circumstance can suffer two interpretations, the apparent and the real.

MOZART

Then speak, sycophant, I know the apparent one. What other reading can this humiliation bear?

THE GRAY STEWARD

It is Death itself that commands you this Requiem. You are to give a voice to all those millions sleeping, who have no one but you to speak for them. There lie the captains and the thieves, the queens and the drudges, while the evening of their earthly remembrance shuts in, and from that great field rises an eternal *miserere nobis*. Only through the intercession of great love, and of great art which is love, can that despairing cry be eased. Was that not sufficient cause for this commission to be anonymous?

MOZART

[*Drops trembling on one knee beside the couch.*]

Forgive me.

THE GRAY STEWARD

And it was for this that the pretext and mover was chosen from among the weakest and vainest of humans. Death has her now, and all her folly has passed into the dignity and grandeur of her state. Where is your pride now? Here are her slippers and her trinkets. Press them against your lips. Again! Again! Know henceforth that only he who has kissed the leper can enter the kingdom of art.

MOZART

I have sinned, yet grant me one thing. Grant that I may live to finish the Requiem.

THE GRAY STEWARD

No! No!

[*And it remains unfinished.*]

HAST THOU CONSIDERED MY SERVANT JOB?

HAST THOU CONSIDERED MY SERVANT JOB?

Now it came to pass on the day when the sons of God came to present themselves before SATAN *that* CHRIST *also came among them. And*

SATAN

[*Said unto* CHRIST.]
Whence comest Thou?

CHRIST

[*Answered* SATAN *and said*]
From going to and fro in the earth, and from walking up and down in it.
[*And*]

SATAN

[*Said unto* CHRIST]
Hast Thou considered my servant Judas? For there is none like him in the earth, an evil and a faithless man, one that feareth me and turneth away from God.
[*Then*]

CHRIST

[*Answered* SATAN *and said*]
Doth Judas fear thee for naught? Hast thou not made a hedge about him, and about his house, and

about all that he hath on every side? But draw back thy hand now and he will renounce thee to thy face.
[*And*]

SATAN

[*Said unto* CHRIST]
Behold, all that he hath is in thy power.
[*So* CHRIST *went forth from the presence of* SATAN.]

* * * * *

[*He descended to the earth. Thirty-three years are but a moment before* SATAN *and before* GOD, *and at the end of this moment* CHRIST *ascends again to His own place. He passes on this journey before the presence of the adversary.*]

SATAN

You are alone! Where is my son Judas whom I gave into your hands?

CHRIST

He follows me.

SATAN

I know what you have done. And the earth rejected you? The earth rejected you! All Hell murmurs in astonishment. But where is Judas, my son and my joy?

CHRIST

Even now he is coming.

SATAN

Even Heaven, when I reigned there, was not so tedious as this waiting. Know, Prince, that I am too proud to show all my astonishment at your defeat. But now that you are swallowing your last humiliation, now that your failure has shut the mouths of the angels, I may confess that for a while I feared you. There is a fretfulness in the hearts of men. Many are inconstant, even to me. Alas, every man is not a Judas. I knew even from the beginning that you would be able, for a season, to win their hearts with your mild eloquence. I feared that you would turn to your own uses this fretfulness that visits them. But my fears were useless. Even Judas, even when my power was withdrawn from him, even Judas betrayed you. Am I not right in this?

CHRIST

You are.

SATAN

You admitted him into your chosen company. Is it permitted to me to ask for how much he betrayed you?

CHRIST

For thirty pieces of silver.

SATAN

[*After a pause.*]

Am I permitted to ask to what rôle he was assigned in your company?

CHRIST

He held its money-bags.

SATAN

[*Dazed.*]

Does Heaven understand human nature as little as that? Surely the greater part of your closest companions stayed beside you to the end?

CHRIST

One stayed beside me.

SATAN

I have overestimated my enemy. Learn again, Prince, that if I were permitted to return to the earth in my own person, not for thirty years, but for thirty hours, I would seal all men to me and all the temptations in Heaven's gift could not persuade one to betray me. For I build not on intermittent dreams and timid aspirations, but on the unshakable passions of greed and lust and self-love. At last this is made clear: Judas, Judas, all the triumphs of Hell await you. Already above the eternal pavements of black marble the banquet is laid. Listen, how my nations are stirring in new hope and in new joy. Such music has not been lifted above my lakes and my mountains since the day I placed the apple of knowledge between the teeth of Adam.

[*Suddenly the thirty pieces of silver are cast upward from the revolted hand of* JUDAS. *They hurtle through the skies, flinging their enormous shadows across the stars and continue falling forever through the vast funnel of space.*

[*Presently* JUDAS *rises, the black stains about his throat and the rope of suicide.*]

SATAN

What have they done to you, my beloved son? What last poor revenge have they attempted upon you? Come to me. Here there is comfort. Here all this violence can be repaired. The futile spite of Heaven cannot reach you here. But why do you not speak to me? My son, my treasure!

[JUDAS *remains with lowered eyes.*]

CHRIST

Speak to him then, my beloved son.

JUDAS

[*Still with lowered eyes, softly, to* SATAN.]

Accursed be thou, from eternity to eternity.

[*These two mount upward to their due place and* SATAN *remains to this day, uncomprehending, upon the pavement of Hell.*]

THE FLIGHT INTO EGYPT

ϒ

THE FLIGHT INTO EGYPT

From time to time there are auctions of the fittings that made up the old Dime Museums, and at such an auction you should be able to pick up a revolving cyclorama of the Holy Land and Egypt, which is the scenery for this piece. Turn down the gas-lights, for it is night in Palestine, and introduce a lady and a child on a donkey. They are accompanied by an old man on foot. The Donkey's name is HEPZIBAH.

HEPZIBAH

[*For the tenth time.*]
I'm tired.

OUR LADY

I know, I know.

HEPZIBAH

I'm willing to carry you as far and as fast as I can, but within reason.

ST. JOSEPH

If you didn't talk so much you'd have more strength for the journey.

HEPZIBAH

It's not my lungs that are tired, it's my legs. When I talk I don't notice how tired I am.

OUR LADY

Do as you think best, Hepzibah, but do keep moving. I can still hear Herod's soldiers behind us.

[*Noise of ironmongery in the wings, right.*]

HEPZIBAH

Well, I'm doing my best.

[*Silence. The Tigris passes on the cyclorama.*]

We must talk or I'll have to halt. We talked over the Romans and the whole political situation, and I must say again that I and every thinking person can only view such a situation with alarm, with real alarm. We talked over the village, and I don't think there's anything more to say about that. Did I remember to tell you that Issachbar's daughter's engagement had been broken?

OUR LADY

Yes.

HEPZIBAH

Well, there's always ideas. I hope I can say honestly that I am at home in ideas of all sorts. For instance, back in the yard I'm the leader of a group. Among the girls. Very interesting religious discussions, I can tell you. Very helpful.

ST. JOSEPH

[*As some more iron is heard falling in Judœa; the Euphrates passes.*]

Can't you hurry a bit?

HEPZIBAH

I always say to the girls: Girls, even in faith we are supposed to use our reason. No one is intended to swallow hook, line and sinker, as the saying is. Now take these children that Herod is killing. Why were they born, since they must die so soon? Can any one answer that? Or put it another way: Why is the little boy in your arms being saved while the others must perish?

ST. JOSEPH

Is it necessary to stop?

HEPZIBAH

I was stopping for emphasis.—Mind you, it's not that I doubt. Honest discussion does not imply doubt necessarily.—What was that noise?

OUR LADY

I beg of you to make all the haste you can. The noise you hear is that of Herod's soldiers. My child will be slain while you argue about Faith. I beg of you, Hepzibah, to save him while you can.

HEPZIBAH

I assure you I'm doing the best I can, and I think I'm moving along smartly. I didn't mean that noise, anyway; it was a noise ahead. Of course, your child is dearer to you than others, but *theologically speaking*, there's no possible reason why you should escape safely into Egypt while the others should be put to the sword, as the Authorized Version has it. When the Messiah comes these things will be made clear, but until then I intend to exercise my reasoning faculty. My theory is this. . . .

OUR LADY

Hepzibah, we shall really have to beat you if you stop so often. Hepzibah, don't you remember me? Don't you remember how you fell on your knees in the stable? Don't you remember my child?

HEPZIBAH

What? What! Of course!

OUR LADY

Yes, Hepzibah.

HEPZIBAH

Let me stop just a moment and look around. No, I don't dare to stop. Why didn't I recognize you before! Really, my lady, you should have spoken more sharply to me. I didn't know I could run like this; it's a pleasure. Lord, what a donkey I was to be arguing about reason while my Lord was in danger.

[*A pyramid flies by.*]

Do you see the lights of the town yet? That's the Sphinx at the right, madam, yes, 3655 B.C. Well, well, it's a queer world where the survival of the Lord is dependent on donkeys, but so it is. Why didn't you tell me before, my lady?

ST. JOSEPH

We thought you could carry us forward on your own merit.

HEPZIBAH

Oh, forgive me, madam; forgive me, sir. You don't hear any more soldiers now, I warrant you. Please don't direct me so far—excuse me—to the right, madam. That's the Nile, and there are crocodiles. My lady, may I ask one question now that we're safe?

OUR LADY

Yes, Hepzibah.

HEPZIBAH

It's this matter of faith and reason, madam. I'd love to carry back to our group of girls whatever you might say about it. . . .

OUR LADY

Dear Hepzibah, perhaps some day. For the present just do as I do and bear your master on.

[*More pyramids fly by; Memnon sings; the Nile moves dreamily past, and the inn is reached.*]

THE ANGEL THAT TROUBLED THE WATERS

THE ANGEL THAT TROUBLED THE WATERS

The Pool.—A vast gray hall with a hole in the ceiling open to the sky. Broad stone steps lead up from the water on its four sides. The water is continuously restless and throws blue reflections upon the walls. The sick, the blind and the malformed are lying on the steps. The long stretches of silence and despair are broken from time to time when one or another groans and turns in his rags, or raises a fretful wail or a sudden cry of exasperation at long-continued pain. A door leads out upon the porch where the attendants of the sick are playing at dice, waiting for the call to fling their masters into the water when the angel of healing stirs the pool. Beyond the porch there is a glimpse of the fierce sunlight and the empty streets of an oriental noonday.

Suddenly the ANGEL *appears upon the top step. His face and robe shine with a color that is both silver and gold, and the wings of blue and green, tipped with rose, shimmer in the tremulous light. He walks slowly down among the shapeless sleepers and stands gazing into the water that already trembles in anticipation of its virtue.*

[*A new invalid enters.*]

THE NEWCOMER

Come, long-expected love. Come, long-expected love. Let the sacred finger and the sacred breath stir up the pool. Here on the lowest step I wait with festering limbs, with my heart in pain. Free me, long-expected love, from this old burden. Since I cannot stay, since I must return into the city, come now, renewal, come, release.

[*Another invalid wakes suddenly out of a nightmare, calling: "The Angel! The Angel has come. I am cured." He flings himself into the pool, splashing his companions. They come to life and gaze eagerly at the water. They hang over the brink and several slide in. Then a great cry of derision rises: "The Fool! Fool! His nightmare again. Beat him! Drive him out into the Porch." The mistaken invalid and his dupes drag themselves out of the water and lie dripping disconsolately upon the steps.*]

THE MISTAKEN INVALID

I dreamt that an angel stood by me and that at last I should be free of this hateful place and its company. Better a mistake and this jeering than an opportunity lost.

[*He sees the* NEWCOMER *beside him and turns on him plaintively.*]

Aïe! You have no right to be here, at all events. You are able to walk about. You pass your days in the city. You come here only at great intervals, and it may be that by some unlucky chance you might be the first one to see the sign. You would rush into the water and a cure would be wasted. You are yourself a physician. You have restored my own children. Go back to your work and leave these miracles to us who need them.

THE NEWCOMER

[*Ignoring him; under his breath.*]

My work grows faint. Heal me, long-expected Love; heal me that I may continue. Renewal, release; let me begin again without this fault that bears me down.

THE MISTAKEN INVALID

I shall sit here without ever lifting my eyes from the surface of the pool. I shall be the next. Many times, even since I have been here, many times the Angel has passed and has stirred the water, and hundreds have left the hall leaping and crying out with joy. I shall be the next.

THE ANGEL

[*Kneels down on the lowest step and meditatively holds his finger poised above the shuddering water.*]

Joy and fulfilment, completion, content, rest and release have been promised.

THE NEWCOMER

Come, long-expected Love.

THE ANGEL

[*Without turning makes himself apparent to the* NEWCOMER *and addresses him.*]

Draw back, physician, this moment is not for you.

THE NEWCOMER

Angelic visitor, I pray thee, listen to my prayer.

THE ANGEL

Healing is not for you.

THE NEWCOMER

Surely, surely, the angels are wise. Surely, O, Prince, you are not deceived by my apparent wholeness. Your eyes can see the nets in which my wings are caught; the sin into which all my endeavors sink half-performed cannot be concealed from you.

THE ANGEL

I know.

THE NEWCOMER

It is no shame to boast to an Angel of what I might yet do in Love's service were I but freed from this bondage.

THE MISTAKEN INVALID

Surely the water is stirring strangely to-day! Surely I shall be whole!

THE ANGEL

I must make haste. Already the sky is afire with the gathering host, for it is the hour of the new song among us. The earth itself feels the preparation in the skies and attempts its hymn. Children born in this hour spend all their lives in a sharper longing for the perfection that awaits them.

THE NEWCOMER

Oh, in such an hour was I born, and doubly fearful to me is the flaw in my heart. Must I drag my shame, Prince and singer, all my days more bowed than my neighbor?

THE ANGEL

[*Stands a moment in silence.*]

Without your wound where would your power be? It is your very remorse that makes your low voice tremble into the hearts of men. The very angels themselves cannot persuade the wretched and blundering children on earth as can one human being broken on the wheels of living. In Love's service only the wounded soldiers can serve. Draw back.

[*He swiftly kneels and draws his finger through the water. The pool is presently astir with running ripples. They increase and a divine wind strikes the gay surface. The waves are flung upon the steps. The* MISTAKEN MAN *casts himself into the Pool, and the whole company lurches, rolls, or hobbles in. The servants rush in from the porch. Turmoil. Finally the no longer* MISTAKEN INVALID *emerges and leaps joyfully up the steps. The rest, coughing and sighing, follow him. The* ANGEL *smiles for a moment and disappears.*]

THE HEALED MAN

Look, my hand is new as a child's. Glory be to God! I have begun again.

[*To the* NEWCOMER.]

May you be the next, my brother. But come with me first, an hour only, to my home. My son is lost in dark thoughts. I—I do not understand him, and only you have ever lifted his mood. Only an hour . . . my daughter since her child has died, sits in the shadow. She will not listen to us. . . .

Sac-City A
F

5